The Garden/er

by

Annie Maclean

First published 2019 by The Hedgehog Poetry Press

Published in the UK by
The Hedgehog Poetry Press
Coppack House, 5
Churchill Avenue
Clevedon
BS21 6QW

www.hedgehogpress.co.uk

ISBN: 978-1-913499-00-6

Extract from *Natural Selection, A Year in the Garden* by Dan Pearson,
by kind permission of Faber & Faber

9 8 7 6 5 4 3 2 1

A CIP Catalogue record for this book is available from the British
Library.

For H.M.   *(7.02.26-27.11.12)*

'It is a place that opens up ease of thought.'

'a single year's experience is like the growth that accompanies it. It builds and layers and enriches.'

Dan Pearson: Natural Selection, A Year in the Garden

Contents

JANUARY

a noticing him
as if remembering him
had recovered him

This present is a harness.
Must there be so much ahead?
From here, there is so much unknown.
Time is glue. It's binding me.
This present waits; it holds me down.

Once upon a time, long ago and far away, deep inside a secret garden, a
snowflake is thrown down from the heavens. It falls upon a ghostly tree
which takes the name as 'silver birch'. Its bark peels back like tissue
paper. Black stripes. As if they're sideways stroked like gestures from a
charcoal painter.

The snowflake sparkles on the trunk. Diamond-white. Glitter-bright. Low
light holds the day's heat down. Ice discs lie like lids on puddles.

Snowflakes swim in spring and become water. The summer sun throws
down its light to let the flakes evaporate. They return inside the autumn's
rain then wait for winter's ice and lace.

Through tales, such circles roll around.

Come: look inside a secret garden to explore what connects the earth to
heaven.

By the end of the year,
he'll lie dead – as he wanted.
I'll keep walking this garden
with love and disdain.

7

January is Janus's month:
the god of beginnings; the god of endings.
The god of the gateways; the doorways for passings.

Time and life are already passing:
January is written as first month on the calendar.
January is named second month of the winter.

The Saxons said it as 'the wolf month':
a bite - a time for cold and darkness.

Feel the space for peace and silence.

Chaucer named his old man 'Januarie':
he described him 'oolde' with 60 years.

                    My father was 'oolder' than Januarie.

I'm facing forward
to walk the garden;
to follow the year.
To find a gateway.

Janus releases eight hours of daylight.
I see sixteen hours of darkness.

After an ending, does the track continue
towards another destination?
Do we follow circles round our cycles,
mindlessly, to reach our deaths?
Are we any better than the beetles,
gorged upon by stripey badgers?
In the garden, on a slant,
a buddha stares out. Commentless.
Already, it seems, we're abandoned by gods.

A teasel stands erect.
A stick in the snow.
A stark monochrome,
desiccated and dead.
Its bristles are crisped
by advancing whisperings
from something that's approaching.
It's whipping the wind.

January nights are ghostly.
A rush of feathers and a hooting.
'it's best to be a living being,
that is, a being who is growing.'

This garden holds the restless ghosts
of ancestors and future deaths.
If time slides along a Mobius strip,
I believe that I can find him here.

Beneath the ice moon,
beside the wolf moon,
the snow lies down
like diamond dust.
Soon it will melt
to meet the next season.

a drive of gravel
as if an irritation
had been quickly scratched

FEBRUARY

a bunch of snowdrops
as if crystal waterglass
had been awakened

On this day in another year
my father
will be '90 years old'.
On this day in another year
my father
will be 'dead for ten years'.

I carry a photograph of
my father
on my phone.
He is three years old and
smiling as the crow flies.
A bonny wee boy.
Shining.
Golden.
He is standing firm,
clutching his pail
on a holiday beach.
His chubby legs
stand browned by the sun.
His hair is sunbleached.

Sometimes I exist on a different dimension
where I stand as a savant.
I know you'll become a gentle man,
loved by a wife and by several communities.
You will lead a long and an honourable life.
You will plant and nurture many gardens.
When you die, you will lie upon your flowers.
Your memory will be cared for
and be carried;
kept in contact.
Unforgotten.

The garden is waking,
thawing from a winter
leaving, which leaving,
leaves puddles.
Perforations of water and ice
formed from drips
to shape ring pulls
display tiny tearings of mosses
in browns, golds and greens.
We kneel down to see
whether life can be living.

Today we will see nine hours of light.

I whisper to the bulbs
which were pricked out in October.
They sleep under the lawn, tucked in and hidden.
I listen for their answers –
for movements or mutterings.
They refuse to be woken.
They stay safe in their slumbers.

The dead remain dead.
When do the living awaken?

The air seems too bright,
like its light has been sharpened.
The damp soil is seeping.
We're harnessed by coldness.
We're waiting and willing
to believe we're not frozen.

Twilight.
Earlier or later, it seems not to matter.
Behind the barren ash tree
on the outline of the garden
there was a tiny shimmering.
A disturbance. An unsettling.
For some inexplicable reason,
this smear, this smudge, was staying.
It lives inside its outline.

> *a sleeping garden*
> *as if scourers with brown leaves*
> *had removed dead skin*

MARCH

a drift of perfume
as if the violets waited
to be cut and crushed

The day had been stretched by two hours.
The trees are untouched by our reference.
They are still swaying, still standing.

the light is thin
hoping the spring
is tasting the year
and
the light is thin
not hoping the spring
is tasting the year

When we are doubtful, we dig.
Earth remembers the winter
and is dark and unyielding.

I see him when the tide is turning,
when the air itself sounds like sighing.
Will he follow the direction of his breath?

Does he wonder who I am
when he meets me on his wanderings?
I do not recognise his eyes.
His unblinking glare sweeps the ground.
His outline is on the edge of melting.

Tomorrow, I must try to find him
to greet him
before the shadows take him.

When the rains rain
on the fantasies of arks and floods,
we remind ourselves that we can swim
though the earth itself seems underwater.
We count the hours
as they cross through each tide table.
We long to see the garden springing.
We bore ourselves,
imagining wild descriptions
of colours and patterns, of the leaves and the petals.

And outside, the winds continue their hissing.

Has autumn already knocked on our door
to advise of the fading of all the snowdrops?
It seems it's so. Time rolls on a torrent.
Time runs on the tide.
Time tracks our treads across the ground
when we search for the snowdrops
through ice and through water.
Yet
the garden is drying; the winds give it an airing.
I hear my mother's approval in a soft exhalation.

> *a drift of perfume*
> *as if the frozen violets*
> *had been thawed and crushed*

APRIL

purple becomes blue
as if tiny ringing bells
had changed register

The season is confused.
Relentless breezes hiss, upsetting tamarisks
which swoop down on pink feathers
to whip up a lashing.

The weather holds a restlessness.
We wait, exhausted and anxious.

Overnight, the grass is luminous.
It is shining.
It gleams like plastic.

A shadow is shuffling of the edge of the garden.
His shallow breaths are familiar.
He manages to hold back his snarling
as he hungers for snowdrops.
Their disappearance will be hunted
till his shadow has faded.

To wake to this morning:
a deep bass beats below the blue
to read descriptions of the day –
mixing colours and perfumes
bathed in the Blues
from its beginnings to its endings
to understand:
everywhere is a beginning;
everywhere becomes an ending.

And new starts happen everywhere.
I find a longer day
to tread the earth,
to touch the ground;
to watch primroses reveal a yellow
softer than the gentlest evening.
They increase their stretching every year.

Cowslips emerge above the wetness,
their yellow brighter than the primrose.
They waken memories of spring.

The ash tree is dry and skeletal.
Its branches reach out grey and naked.
No evidence of life returning.
I forget it takes its time to waken.
I want to cut it down.
It stretches Death.

I stand to face the Western Wind,
whispering: hiss here this orison to heaven:

listen to the brush of bluebells.
Stroke their softness. Note their movement.
Catch the pivot of their breathing.
Watch as they become a song.
Bless this garden after winter.
Let life be welcomed, Death be gone.

At night I dream of shades and darkness.

In the morning I rush to enter the garden.
The dew waits to be drunk.
I think it best to be with the living;
enjoying colour and perfume
and be encouraged to bloom.

a tiny raindrop
as if a thirsty season
had sighed and wakened

MAY

a long plot of grass
as if a flattened table
hid below velvet

On the slant appear aquilegia
with bells of violets and faded pinks.
They follow the flagstones down to the gate.
They're standing still, and still they're waiting.
There is a fine memory:
One early May. One quiet morning
when the clear sky seemed to summon hope,
I walked down towards the woods,
parting the soft bells which stroked my waist.
I felt the first warmth of the sun
which invited in the early bees
to drink the colours and their nectar.
Here the world seemed untouched and novel.
The bells lean and want to sing for me.

Now, at the edging of the lawn
where the soft grass isn't velvet,
shaded by the rowan's branches
stands a grey man.
Unfocussed.
Shuffling.
Like a shadow disappearing.
In his hands he holds a hoe
which he rakes across the soil
and shakes his head
for something lost.
His sigh sounds like a sough of wind.

I remember my father in his garden.
He pointed to the columbine
which he had nursed from tiny seeds.
This flower was a secret for my mother.
He anticipated her surprise.

21

'I love to grow this aquilegia.
It's name is teased as "Granny's Bonnet"'.
He shook his head and stroked the petals.
'It reminds me of a pansy's face.'
He pointed out the owl-like eyes.
I admired its milky petals
surrounded by its spears of violet.

He promised he would gather seeds
to send when I returned to exile.
'In early May, greet the pansy-face;
it once lived in a Highland garden.'

the flat black night sky
as if every point of light
had abandoned light

JUNE

a sycamore tree
as if the tidal seaweed
stands in a current

0430 hrs.
The sun is rising on the magpies
as they begin to rasp and grate.
Their ricochets resemble lightning,
zigzagging across the tops of trees.
They swoop through air like pterodactyls,
down to bounce on velvet grass.

There should be sound.

Two seagulls stamp upon a roof
and stare at anything that moves.
They are guarding eggs within their nest,
sheltered from prevalent breezes
behind an unused chimney pot.

On the open patio
sea pinks push between the flagstones.
Here the air is coarsely scented
by the closeness of the ocean.
Repetition of the hissing waves
is hypnotic as they hit the shingle.
Terns tread the shallows of the sea-foam.

Here we watch and search the sounds.

Cross-legged
barefoot
concentrating
punching holes in daisy stems
fantasies of being a fairy
seven years old
what hopes ahead?

Time pitters past on tiny raindrops ....

Today the old man is in focus.
He brings his hand outside his pocket
and peers upon his outstretched palm
to see the cheese that he has hidden
to throw down to a friendly robin
who watches as he hoes the garden.

But he looks shaken ...

He sees that this is not his garden.
Inside this month, there is no robin.
It seems that his home has been hidden.
He peers again upon his palm.
Bewildered by now-empty pockets,
he returns to find his out-of-focus.

It's mid-month. The wind has strengthened.
This season feels blown.
Droopy leaves upon the trees look burned -
or maybe desiccated.
Shining clouds hold up the sky
and could explode at any second
like balloons whose skins are too far inflated.
They are holding light behind the white.
It is too bright to maintain tension.

A Beauty Bush. Amabilis.
A pink cloud made from tiny bells
whose yellow throats
open wide to sing
that they feel celebratory.
The bush becomes a bride's bouquet.
A cascade to stroke and sweep the ground.
By mid-June it will be blown away
by the scorching and the hissing winds.

Poppies are thinning. Velvet and crimson.
Elementals are beating up the garden.

This is a massacre.
Beauty is failing.

Seagulls sway like paper planes
held from above on lines of thread.
Is this how they learn to fly,
sweeping, swooping, between the thermals?

There was a time the grass grew velvet
and daisies were the 'days' eyes'.
Buttercups reach to offer up their yellow,
then came the time for dandelions.
The bumble bees bounced over heathers
and dived deep within the blousy mallows.
The garden was a place to play;
to imagine horses reading thoughts
in the gleam of sunlight. Glorious.

> I remember my father in his garden
> fighting the harshness from the ocean
> which scorched through the thinness of the soil
> stretched out across the granite.
> He grew his garden as a gift
> to please his wife, to make her smile
> (for she loved snowdrops and the robins).
> Through every window she could watch him
> pricking out seeds into a pattern
> to catch colours for her admiration.

In another land, I live a different life.
This garden opens to the seasons.
We hoe against the thorns and weeds
and watch the bees hum over meadows.
Here nature selects the vegetation.

a night of dreaming
as if all our adventures
had been plotted out

JULY

*an open new month
as if a cacophony
had bloomed in colours*

overnight
the wind blows out
removing all the irritation

a wren sings as though she's underwater

Beneath the sun
the spurge looks alien
with branches like fir
and leaves like squashed clover.
Fluorescent bright lime
is highlighted with crimson.
(Kids laugh they look like tiny bottoms.)
Tomorrow
 we'll wait for them to pop
as they spit out their seeds
in the hope they'll be scattered.

Inspired by aliens
fractals of the fennel's fronds
suddenly seem to be suspicious –
their green's to thin; too luminous.

          The outline of the shaking man
          has relocated to the shadow
          to avoid the scalpel of the sun
          I fear he's dank; unsavoury.
          I ask him: 'Have you lost your name?'
          He peers back at me, uncomprehending.

          Is it too early for a spider's web?
          I feel I cannot sever him.
          Something sticky holds me on.
          I dread any future revelation.

If colours could sing,
they'd giggle outrageously.
Red valerian is pink footprints –
tiny sparrow-markings dancing.
Five-petalled purple on verbena
stretch up thin stems, reaching skyward.

There are possibilities in elastic height.

Tumbled petals. Over-spilled.
Blueberry blues, tomato reds,
custard yellows and ice-white geraniums.
Poppy statues stand up. Blazing.
The crescendo of the symphony
screams too light – beyond our hearing.

When I was small
I learned the names of colours
from oblongs nestling on my paint-box
or crayons in my pencil case.
Now I paint rainbows
which I flood out with washes.
I'm trying to trace the messages of colours.

a garden shining
as if tiny temple bells
had been softly stroked

AUGUST

necklaces of rain
as if an unsettled night
had tugged at diamonds

Throughout the night
flashings slid across the skies.
Pulsations shone into the clouds.
This storm was powerful
and silent.
Spooky – and what caused this light?
It felt as though our ears were broken.

Had the aliens arrived?

Now, watch:
the trees stretch out their leaves.
They spread their elongated fingers.
A mist is sticking to the branches,
clutching spray.
Enormous. Lambent.

The garden
helps the shine
of an early dawn
to exhale its light.
I observe it as a radiance.

Does this mirror Eden's garden?
Here the pause.
Here the pivot.
Here the luminescence.

When I awake,
things look on the slant.
The viburnum has grown taller.
Its flowers are unearthly:
uncountable petals
sucking at something
immobile and unseen
from inside the air.

I lean closer to listen.
Is there a hissing?

August holds the longest light
but the air is cooling. The year is changing.
Dragonflies seem prehistoric
in size and intention
as they hover and follow the wasps round the garden.

Spiders scuttle after midnight
and the cats wait to point to them with their claws.
We find the corpses in the morning.
We dare not touch them. We dread their spasms.

The swifts are quick to snatch at insects.
They're tealeaves thrown across the sky.
They're being urged to venture south
to where warmth protects the land from winter.

There's a last blaze of colour in this season:
viper's bugloss is bold in blue
and pink cyclamen appears again
to prove the air can still be tender.
Japanese anemones are creamy white;
stopped spinning plates of ceramic plaster.
Evening primrose shows a powdered yellow
with a magnolia mix. A softest whisper.

To where does he disappear
at night?
Does he choose to turn to dust
or reform as mist?

At night
I hear the garden breathing.
Its covering of green is moving.
I can feel a rush of oxygen.
Something huge is going on
deep within the black. Unseen.
The leaves are rustling on the poplar.
I close my eyes to wait for light.

a ripple of shade
as if a winter duvet
had been remembered

SEPTEMBER

a pointillist disc
as if a poplar's glitter
had been shivering

Watch: the papery leaves flutter on the poplar. They are:

Cinerous	griseous	whey
virescent	chlorochrous	lovat
flavescent	citrine	jessamy

Watch: the leaves are twinkling on the poplar. They are:

Sarcoline	virid	celadon
topaz	tawny	wheaten
greige	eburnean	argent

Watch: the leaves are sparkling on the poplar. They are:

suede	chartreuse	lutescent
sage	porraceous	prasinous
melichrous	primrose	citreous

Watch: the leaves are quavering on the poplar. They are:

zinnober	chrysochlorous	viridian
luteolous	xanthic	ochre
olivaceous	lovat	caesious

Watch: the leaves are quivering on the poplar. They are:

columbine	watched	cresious
hoary	liard	isabelline
fulvous	luteous	sulphureous

Watch: the leaves are sparkling on the poplar.

Hear: the sea beyond the garden.

And the ocean is cerulean
           it is cyneous
           it is glaucous

Listen: the air is shuddering.

The waves are breaking on the shingle.
They sound as if the water's cracking.

One can swim inside the water.
The groynes can cut the flesh like limpets.
Two seals, observers from a distance,
have four limpid eyes and shark-sharp teeth.
It's safer to swim in familiar channels
- like evading webs inside the garden.

The cooler air is hanging round
in spaces in this garden.

        If I could see him returning home,
        he'd be raking leaves and teaching me
        about actinomycetes, nitrogen,
        the smell of brown, the life in earth.

There is bistort beside the lower gate.
We call it 'mountain fleece'
and by other warm names: 'Fire Dance' and 'Fire Tail'.
Its stems are far too skinny; spikey. Ready spears?
It grows too fast and glows too rosy.
Its pointed leaves clasp round its stalk.

Suddenly, this seems too weird.
Nature looks unnatural.
Flavescent leaves don't smell of lemons.

a leaf floating down
as if an exhalation
had gold and silence

OCTOBER

a leaf then a leaf
as if scents of the season
had rhymed with orange

My father searched Egypt
for goddesses and traditions.
He knew the Great River
which holds back the deserts.
He conversed with men
who sit down cross-legged
to stare at the water;
to translate its currents.
These men read the River.

Now, searching this garden
for gods, explanations,
I listen to the seasons
which demonstrate our patterns.
The watchers of sheep
were driven murderous by Pan
and they tore apart Echo.
But the Earth treasured her music.
This my third day of checking
to look at the sky
for panic and speed:
I hear nothing in the silence.
The swifts have moved on.

At the back are the woods
where the great trees are standing.
Chestnuts and sycamores.
Huge, high and motionless.
If I too stay still,
I can hear their leaves falling.
Gentle, light whispers
which float down to ground.
Alone, I witness all of this happening.

This is the season of decay and of rust.
There is a smouldering of colour.
Red bleeds into yellow.
Pyrocantha, thorns of fire,
is orange and poisonous.
Its needles clutch like fish hooks.
In the bareness of the night,
a fox tiptoes the garden,
screaming at the sky; screeching at everything.

October can be seen as the first month of spring.
The cycle begins underground
where the worms tidy up what is rotting
and clean out the earth.
The badgers follow along their ancient pathways
to gorge on windfalls and worms.

>My father told me his hard tales of nature
>about dogs eating dogs
>to satisfy hunger.

The air smells of decay.
There are strong, sticky webs
enormous spiders have woven
to suck the life from the living.
Overhead the geese are barking,
returning to their winter beds.

>I can see my father smirking
>on his situation
>in the embers of the autumn.

>*a life as a leaf*
>*as if winter approaching*
>*had torn off a life*

October is disappearing.
The veil between the lands walked by the living
and the unseen spaces shared by the dead
is less than threadbare.
The dimensions are losing their thickness of outline.
The air is empty.
The dark is welcome.

Has my father already met with my dead mother?
In his shadow, he's outlined clearer.
His footsteps sound softer.
His breathing is lowered;
slower and deepened.

He has made his decision
to sever an anchor.
He will cast off from his life.

From now on, he'll be distant.

Why won't he listen?

a leaf then the leaves
as if the undressed branches
had shaken their arms

NOVEMBER

an open garden
as if the watching robins
knew the ways to leave

The Scorpionic month.
In this month, I was born.
In this month, you will die.

The Mystics painted on their scrolls for Scorpio
stars symbolising time, connection,
when Dark Matter flows along dimensions.

It's like you stroll down
to open the garden gates
to watch the robins
crossing the seasons.

We sat with you
to count your breathing,
to be beside you
and let it happen.

I didn't note your final words
but I watched the grace
of your last breath.

I felt your spirit disappear.

Nothing left for us
but a pause for peace.

an easy last breath
as if something sacred
could gently vanish

We both entered into new dimensions.

I saw:
first the ceiling
then the four walls
and next the flooring

ripped
scoured
stripped
of comfort
or recognisable covering

noiselessly

We were stuck in shock,
abandoned by you.

*a room filled with space
as if there was nothing left
but silence frozen*

When I think of you,
I think of you as a gardener.

I remember your purest smile
which reminds me of my photo
of you as a child,
happy on your holiday.
I think of you holding a wheelbarrow,
gathering molehills
or planting heathers for the bees.
Spade in hand,
you dig the soil
to welcome the worms.

I am hungry for these memories.

After your 'elevenses',
you slice up some cheese
to hide in your pocket
to share with the birds.

Robins ate from your palm.
We believed you held magic.

the gardens you dug
as if all the worms wriggling
escaped the robins

The ancestors taught us our rituals:
On observing a death,
one should open a window
so as not to block progress.

Does a soul wait behind
for the rush from outside
before it departs?

So, where did you go?

I hope it is bright.

a window opened
as if your spirit waited
to enter the light

DECEMBER

a second of time
as if all the universe
had discontinued

Dark December. Damp and weighted.
The colours leached.

Could light be fractured by the wind?

On a good day, eight hours of light
gleam thinly.
This is the month of suicides.

> *'He always was competitive.*
> *I expected him to be ahead.*
> *Second does not win the race.'*
> These are the words my grandmother taught him.

> ... so he'd tried to overtake his death...

> He would be the cause of his own ending.
> He would leave his life with determination
> and not wait the uncertainties of fate.

I denied that this could happen.

> I read him '*Ozymandias*'
> when we tracked over the River
> for crocodile traces.

> And I whisper those lines
> when I stand by his graveside.

> For me, he stood '*a King of Kings*'.
> I crouch, a carrier of despair.

The garden lies in monochrome.

'Nothing beside remains. Round the decay
of that colossal wreck, boundless and bare'

    - He's moved away.

The rain is turning into snowflakes.
Silently.
Like eiderdown.

                    a garden waiting
                    as if its unborn snowdrops
                    had been abandoned

Something colder is approaching.

I know the slowness of his gait.
At last I recognise his face.

       I see him smile and hear him say:
       'This is the finest snow – it's shining!'
       There's too much that I want to ask.
       I stand still. I reach out.
       I'm silent.

       He says this year is going to change.
       I hear his crunch of surer steps.
       He turns to leave. No footprints follow.

I think:

It's OK if you fade.
Come back next year.
We'll walk together.
We'll watch the garden going round.
I'll show you where the apples fall,
beside the ways the badgers follow.
We've time ahead.
You cannot leave me.
I'll always find your presence here,
even if I cannot see you.

and:

I hope you're OK where you are
and that my mother's there to lead you.
I think that I can let you go
and wish you well;
she's waiting for you.

December turns the cycle round.
It gifts a longing for the future.

In January, I'll search to find you here.
We'll begin again
and do it better.

a clock overwound
as if Northern winds sifted
white across a noise

NOTES

(p.8) Chaucer, Geoffrey *The Canterbury Tales: The Merchant's Tale*

(p.9) a re-translation from Capek, Karel *The Gardener's Year*

(p. 45) Shelley, Percy Bysshe

ACKNOWLEDGMENTS

My thanks to:

Gina, the Centre, the Guardian of the Garden;

Vicky Mackenzie, the Hoer of the Materials;

Mark Davidson for taking a chance;

the Silver Birches who are among the first to appear after a trauma.